BLUE AMEN

BLUE AMEN

Poems

Susan Mallory

ISBN 978-1-09832-026-3

FOR MY FAMILY

"When you think about it from the context of the universe . . .
the earth is only a small, pale bluespot [sic].

Anonymous researcher

Korean Astronomy and Space Science Institute

South Korea

CONTENTS

KIRK WHALUM

plays All Saints Church. His lithe body
bends missionary style

into the curve of the saxophone,
eyes narrow as his cheeks

fill and empty into seamless bursts
of rich sound.

We stiff Episcopalians are slightly
seduced. Discreet toe tapping.

A few shoulders sway. Here and there
hands clap silently. This is a musical first.

Above the altar, Gabriel, horn to lips,
rides a cloud toward the Virgin Mary

robed in her usual blue. Joseph's hand
rests tentatively on her shoulder,

a gesture as disconcerting as Whalum's
final two notes. Middle C to D flat.

HYMN SING

The old folks sat on mismatched chairs
while the kids tumbled Uncle David's floor.

Miss Ethel Gentry, organist from the village church,
played the upright. Her helmet of gray curls

(with a wash of blue) bobbed in time to each hymn
while her fingers hurried the keys to keep up

with the singers' impatience. Grandfather would select
someone to turn pages for Miss Ethel who indicated

when with a chin lift and raised brows. We sang
the same favorites every Sunday night except for

the time Uncle Hugo commandeered the piano
with a booming *move over Miss Ethel let me show 'em*

some honesta goodness singin'. His thick fingers
flapped the keyboard as he growled *oh when the saints.*

I remember Mom telling me when Uncle Hugo asked
Aunt Alice's father for her hand in marriage

he had declared *you New Englanders could really use*
some south of the Mason-Dixon.

BLACKBERRY BLOSSOMS

Chris knows his banjo
like he knows his ancestors
and his place. Kentucky.

His music and poems
are of real stuff, rooted
like the cedar tree he describes

growing out of his grandma's
chest from her grave
not far from where we are.

He's proud of his banjo. It's old.
Made in Boston, 1890. Five strings.
Fingerprints of others worn

into the neck. Small. Made for
high class ladies to play in fancy
parlors. This fact tickles him.

Beneath an old tulip poplar
we listen to him strum and sing.
The setting is right.

Wearing his suede fedora,
blue jay feather stuck
in the band, his tan boot taps

the grass while he sings about
blackberry blossoms
and the Cumberland Gap.

GRAN'S DREAM

I know a long time ago you were young.
In sepia photos I've seen you wave

from a galloping palomino and kick up
your naughty heels in the flapper dress

we have in the dress up closet. Now
your white hair is cropped, the little palm tree

atop your head tied with a thin white ribbon
the way I've tied your first great-gran's wisps

for our visit. There is a span of 1 year plus 100
between you two, each bundled and speechless.

Even so I hear your Quaker *thee-ing* and *thou-ing,*
predictable as triple time in a Strauss waltz

which reminds me of the dream you once told me.

*I am wearing my favorite green chiffon dress. It billows when I
twirl 1 2 3 1 2 3 to "The Blue Danube." My knees work. My feet
don't hurt. My partner is a broomstick because all the boys have
gone to war.*

HELEN FRANKENTHALER'S COLORS

Vermillion puddles
then nips and gnaws at
powder blue which bleeds
unabashedly lavender.

Obliques of persimmon
and ripe plum invade white
which waits unprimed to accept
whatever comes its way.

Emerald green and topaz tango
toward robin's egg blue,
threatening to muddy.
Instead, there's a cooling down.

The colors of Gran's pretty
garnet and grey pearly brooch
trickle   flow   gather speed
before colliding with a serious edge.

AT THE READY

When Mom and Dad moved Grandmother
downstairs to the dining room
the pine table and cane chairs went
to the storage shed to make room
for her bed and bureau.

Now we ate meals in the kitchen
or outside if the flies weren't biting.
I no longer earned a penny a time
easing her feet into sensible brogues

with the elephant ivory shoe horn
her father carved when he was a boy.
Although the windows facing the harbor
were painted shut, she wore a hairnet

just as she did aboard the *Horizon Bound*
to keep her hair from mussing in the wind.
She preferred to sit upright in the narrow bed
my granddaughter sleeps in now.

Hair well secured, shoulders wrapped tight
in a wool shawl, and blue canvas boating shoes
beside the bed she was ready for an east wind
to pick her up at any moment and sail her away.

5.3.1.

Grandfather was in his element admonishing
his grandchildren. He forbade sandy shoes, crumbling
cookies, and sticky candy on board the *Horizon Bound*.
Life jackets must be cinched take your breath away tight.

The summer my brother turned 12 Grandfather appointed
him Chief Supply Officer. It was a job to be both
proud of and scared of.

Before others came aboard he would check
against a handwritten list:

bilge pump
binoculars
fog horn
foul weather gear
Lucky Strikes
a box of blue tipped wood matches
Planter's Peanuts
spare battens
spare anchor
the whistle

Like a policeman
Grandfather blew warnings
on his gnawed black whistle.

5   all aboard
3   raise the mainsail
1   underway

FIRST WATCH

Grandfather demonstrates by swiveling his neck
how my sister is supposed to scan 180 degrees.
She flattens her stomach on the bow deck.

I stay out of the way. She and I are buckled
in orange life jackets covered with mildew as nasty
grey as the fog wrapping the boat.

Grandfather is at the helm.

We wallow in a following sea.
The flap of slack sails and throaty
who who of the Southern Lighthouse
create an eerie duet.

She wears his whistle around her neck
prepared to follow the instructions she repeated
back to him twice before we came aboard.

1 long	boat in sight
2 short	ledges or rocks
short-long-short	close to shore

Every few minutes he hollers *See anything?*

She tells me later she saw a windjammer under full sail
two Indians paddling a birch bark canoe
a pirate ship with cannons lined up across the bow
a blue tailed mermaid riding the back of a killer whale.

But she answers   *no   nothing   not a thing.*

TIDES

We cousins must wait for high tide
to sail across The Ledges and for dead low
to dig clams. That's about all we knew.

Grandfather's explanation of the tides
was complicated and confused us.
We decided the man in the moon

had something to do with it.
Uncle Hugo claimed six loud finger snaps
signaled the six-hour change.

But whose fingers snapped?
We knew fabled King Canute had failed
with a wave of his jeweled scepter

to save his kingdom from a rising tide.
When the waters had drenched his boots
and the hem of his blue tunic he threw

his scepter and his crown into the sea.
When I asked Mom about tides she shook
her head and shrugged a *beats me honey*.

SEARCHING

The sleek red kayak slices the water
leaving an untraceable path above a world
of sea cucumbers and spiny sea urchins.
Alternating left side right she paddles
against the outgoing tide toward Clark Island.

Beaching the boat, she gathers camping gear
and barefoot picks a way through beds
of blue mussels and mounds of clams dropped
and eaten by gulls. Slowed by slick seaweed
she stops to ask herself why the need

to overnight on an uninhabited island.
Could it be the same as the dive off the dinghy
last summer when she'd held her breath until
she couldn't and kicked up for air
hoping she would somehow be different?

PEAHEN'S LAMENT

Feathers are everywhere.
Royal blue, Kelly green, iridescent copper

swirl on the pond scum of pollen
brighten the tans of last fall's

mums and asters. Black eyes on tall plumes
tangle with sharp holly and mahonia leaves.

Bits of rusty red fox fur reveal
the whole sad story.

The peahen's elongated squawks pierce
the quiet of early mornings. She checks

their usual places: roof tops, fence rows,
trees in the meadow. She must remember

his strut and the rattle and shimmy of
quills when he presented his fanned tail,

a frenzied semicircular love invitation
insistent and rhythmic like dry seeds

in a gourd shaken hard by a dancer.
I, too, miss his splendor.

MAGIC

Only one time did he pull a blue parakeet
out of the same black velvet bag
scruffed dingy like the rabbit who
usually emerged while she pretended
to be surprised.

Today is a day with clouds combed stringy
across a dull sky, the sort of day to succumb
to violin-sad or roam to a night last summer
under a new moon on a beach when
she'd wished he would conjure two into one.

STILL LIFE WITH MAGPIES

She looks through the window
framed by stucco walls that cast
a warm glow from the corner kiva.

Bare branches of honey locusts twist
and turn beyond the glass. Magpies
fly in bursts of black and blue

from tree to tree. In the distance
pasture grasses and low bushes
appear to sprout before her eyes

as if a plein air painter were dabbing
shades of green to the beat of the drops
of rain tapping on the roof.

DAY'S END

The hot late afternoon wind dances
the dandelions, their golden globes
deceptively fragile.

It trembles the seed filled heads
of Queen Anne's lace,
spreading their future abundance.

Blue-black ravens, their talons wrapped
on cottonwood branches,
scout their surroundings for creatures

dead or alive. Mountains to the east
gradually darken to a familiar silhouette.
Those to the west are radiant with sunset.

We drive home toward the afterglow
arriving as the stars begin their shine
in the clear night sky.

MOOSE

With polarized focus I see a rainbow trout
hanging near the opposite bank. Blue damselflies
like tiny helicopters fly in all directions
looking for insects over the narrow stream.

It isn't until the trout rises to gulp a damselfly
caught on the surface of the water
that I see a moose standing in the bulrushes on
the opposite bank. He is looking across at me.

His antlers, wide and flat, wing off his head.
His mahogany rump mimics a distant slope.
Like an ugly piece of Victorian furniture
in a too small room he overwhelms the landscape.

SNOW COVER

I prefer winter and fall when you feel the bone structure of
the landscape, the loneliness of it, the dead feeling of winter.
Something waits beneath, the whole story doesn't show.
                                        Andrew Wyeth

Without a hint of sun or blue the snow and wind
on a January day in Yellowstone Park alter
my friends snowshoeing ahead into a vague wash
of unidentifiable figures. They appear, disappear,

and reappear as if within a Wyeth landscape.
His worlds, coastal Maine and Chadds Ford,
so different yet painted with the same palette
as here in Wyoming. Greys, browns, and black

bleed into the snowy landscape much like his drybrush
and egg tempera on white paper.
I find myself within the same isolation he paints.
Now and then through the swirling snow I glimpse

other creatures going about the business of survival.
An eagle spirals down upon what must be a kill.
A group of elk moves with uncommon haste
through snowdrifts, a sign of a wolf pack in pursuit.

A fox buries his nose in the snow. His red tail splayed
across white startles the muted landscape as did
Wyeth's secret portraits of Helga startle the art world.

Helga's luxurious red hair spilling unrestrained across
sumptuous pale breasts and belly like the spreading
tail of the fox as he tugs and pulls up a field mouse.

THE ELK

I hear my ragged breath and the crunch of blue
early morning snow beneath my snowshoes.

I am slogging up a slope shadowed by looming granite
crags as yet untouched by the sun. I stop a moment

in the cold silence. I am alert, a little afraid.
I continue up the incline (I want a view of the valley)

until it flattens. Here I chance upon an elk
sprawled on its side, bloodied, half-devoured.

A line of yellow urine rings him. There are red stains
and chunks of hair all about. Tracks lead to a nearby

stand of pines. Wolves. They must be there
waiting until hunger compels them again.

I abandon my intention and hurry down.
I'll return in summer to collect some elk bones.

I love bones chalked clean by wind and sun, especially
femurs and lower jaws with well-worn teeth.

TORNADO ALLEY

I catch my breath gliding
the flat splendor
of Oklahoma.

I had not expected beauty
in the stagnant pewter
of roadside ditches

or mirrored farm ponds
fringed with lush grass.
It is spring.

Across the landscape
calves tuck into
grazing mothers.

A blue window
in a cloud bank ahead
opens toward Albuquerque.

Later, backlit
by the setting sun,
clouds reshape

a dog's head
a volcano
wings

of a condor
or an archangel
announcing

miles of feed lots
I am passing.
Masses of dark shapes

fenced tight churn the earth.
The foul stench
catches my breath.

I pray these creatures
will be cleansed and freed
by wind swept slaughter.

EXTRA EYES

The paper mache mask of a Hindu goddess
hangs above our bed by two thin cotton strings
threaded through her ear lobes.
The loopy signature of the Balinese maker
embellishes the reverse cavity.

Feathered brows arch the goddess' almond eyes
outlined in turquoise blue and mint green,
the same as trace her elegant nose, ears,
and full red lips. Three more eyes adorn
each creamy cheek. A ninth is in the cleft of her chin.

The mask maker explained a loftier god had created
this goddess with nine eyes to help him detect
and deflect corrupting spirits who, like arrows,
targeted his believers. A deity who acknowledges
his own limitations, this is my kind of theology.

A STONE FOR LUCY

A purple stone shimmering the sunlit shallow
of the Kootenai River was irresistible.
You detected a little pink, as well, when later
you dropped it into a bucket of water.

You witnessed the transforming power of water,
how dry dull can be brought back to dazzle.
I want you to keep this stone, not as a talisman,
but to remember other shared water wonders.

Thirsty bluebells beside creeks, sea creatures
in tidal pools, the sharp point of an icicle.
To remember our granny talks about tsunamis
and earthquakes, droughts and wasting water,

the serious consequences of polluting,
and, even if tempting, not to take a shortcut
off a well-marked trail to follow a waterfall's
tantalizing sound you can hear before you see it.

WALKING FROM MEMPHIS TO RAVENNA

Warm air, moist at last,
clings like sleeves of silk
to my bare arms.

I breathe wet dust.
A delicious smell
forgotten in the long dry.

I sip honeysuckle
tangled in roadside privet.
A sweet revival of appetite.

I swing my arms freely,
feet gliding shiny pebbles
embedded in asphalt.

I remember the mosaics
of glittering blue dolphins
cavorting with Poseidon.

I felt buoyant in Ravenna.

ROAD KILL

Its angular head is mashed, the rest intact.
Filtered sunlight flickers the patterned shapes

on the body. At first, I give wide berth
then decide to double back and pick up

the snake with a long stick. It hangs harmless
but I'm afraid to touch. Primeval fear

like fear of fire or the ocean's undertow,
maybe something vaguely biblical.

Not far away a blue jay feasts on a squirrel
whose four stiff legs point to the sky.

Dead creatures and wild lilies thrive
this time of the year alongside the road.

THE ROAD RISES

We are on the way to the Sayil, site plan in hand,
to photograph Mayan ruins of the Grand Palace,
Mirador Complex, and Ballcourt built by
ancestors of those who in Merida this morning
served us breakfast and filled up our jaunty blue car.

We turn off the highway onto a narrow road.
Two hundred feet ahead the road changes suddenly
from dirt to a color more vivid than a ripe lime.
We slow down, try to figure out what is happening.
The wind from behind has carried the engine noise.

As if responding to the downbeat of a symphony
conductor's baton, the road rises and undulates
like a magic carpet out of the *Arabian Nights.*
Next it breaks up into countless flecks tumbling
like confetti before reconfiguring into a flying wave

that vanishes behind a nearby grove of trees.
We get out of the car, take a few steps, find ourselves
walking on a carpet of lifeless left-behind butterflies.
Our hiking boots silently crush their soft wings. We
nod in disappointed agreement and go no further.

EARLY MORNING

Scoured clear by sleep my mind prowls and strays
between wake up and get up.

I twist and play with words. Won knight eye sale
the sees two ah knew whirled wear peephole . . .

or rewrite and whisper-sing a favorite song.
Somewhere over a cypress or a redwood or a pine . . .

I plant blue peonies in a fantasy garden with daffodils
and zinnias and chrysanthemums blooming all together.

I ponder how my older daughter who I labored long hours
to birth possesses abundant patience

and takes her time to make a decision. Her sister, however,
came into the world in an easy hurry and is quick to decide.

I spread my fingers wide to let fistfuls of sand slip through
noticing how my empty hand has become an hourglass.

THE GARDENER

Our family calls him *El Grande* because he is.
For many years he has worked around our place.
We share a garden. He grows tomatillos, chayote,

serrano and habanero peppers, vegetables he likes.
He tends our arugula, okra, turnip greens, Japanese
eggplant, vegetables foreign to him.

He makes it clear that our string beans and butter beans
are not his kind of *frijoles.* Along the fence he plants
blue potato vines because they are *muy bonitas, Señora.*

Today *El Grande* works from a ladder propped against
the gutter. While I stand below to steady him, he scoops
out leaves sopped and clumped from last night's rain.

We are discussing in general *la condición* of the gutters
when abruptly he leans out toward the magnolia tree
beside the roof and breaks off a blossom.

With an operatic gesture he sweeps it to his chest,
lowers his head to inhale the sweet, gazes up
as if toward heaven and then down to me, and smiles.

His straight white teeth blaze against his bronze skin.
Wearing *sombrero, huaraches,* and old work pants rolled
to calf he's a figure come alive from a Diego Rivera mural.

VICTORY GARDEN

The first of those strange shadowed summers
Mom put us to work digging a garden.
Counting aloud she paced off a perfect square
and blue flagged each corner.
She gave us each a tool, short handled
shovel, sharpshooter, and hoe.

These same tools often worked their way
into stories about childhood summer visits
to her uncle's farm north of Baton Rouge.
In Louisiana dry stalks of corn whispered
secrets in the breeze and spit out seeds
grew watermelons right before your eyes.

Hoping to cultivate the same sort of wizardry
we began to turn over soil. At every stab
and poke metal struck granite. The tools bucked
out of our hands. Mom, who always had told us
finish what you start, for once said *ok quit*
and sent us to Webster's to look up *stratigraphy.*

WAR MOVES

Grownups talked day and night about what might happen.
Volunteers searched for enemy boats thought to be sneaking
into uninhabited coves along the Maine coast. Soon we moved to
Washington, D.C. where blackouts were a nightly reminder and
random air raid sirens hurried us five flights to the basement to
wait for the All Clear Signal. After that we moved to San Diego,
the ship out city. Barbed wire, like a giant stretched out slinky,
lined the beach, fencing in the families who waited. No swimming
or way to reach wet sand to build forts to help protect. Instead
we played lookout searching for periscopes of subs and our dads
who were somewhere in the distant blue beyond the pods of
gray whales heading to Baja to give birth. At school there were
bomb drills and at home keep-quiet dinners while we listened to
war news. One evening the low radio voice was different. Loud
and excited it repeated over and over *the war is over.* "The Star-
Spangled Banner" filled the room. Mom stood up. We followed. I
covered my heart. My hand buttery from eating corn on the cob
left a lasting imprint.

CIRCA 1949

She lets herself in the back door,
breathes in the hush and cool
and smell of lemon furniture wax.
She tosses her book bag on the counter

kicks off blue and white saddle oxfords
and sock skates
to her room and bedside radio.
Soon she is teetering on a high wire

under the Big Top of Clyde Beaty's Circus.
Next, she heads north to the Yukon,
the land of whistling wind,
where she battles ice and snow

with Sky King and the Royal Mounties.
At 6:00 o'clock she follows Boston Blackie
down spooky streets to get the bad guys
before arriving at the dinner table at 6:30.

5TH GRADE

Writing math problems on the board
the untamed frizzy hair and large bottom
of the formidable Miss Agnes Schnebly
were especially notable. When the recess

bell rang and, if we'd behaved, we were free.
Ann Simpson would toe trace hopscotch
squares in the freshly swept playground dirt.
The dust when we jumped made sunny puffs.

I remember most everything about 5th grade.

My brother's friend Will Craig, a red headed
6th grader with a field of face freckles, tried
to hold my hand in the cafeteria line.

Danny Taylor, tall and pigeon toed, stood
picking his nose when he forgot the verse
he was reciting from "Paul Revere's Ride."

My best friend Janet's father died in a crash.
A drunk driver speeding on the freeway
rear-ended his new blue Thunderbird.

Grownups said the way he died was ironical.
Ironical was a word none of us knew, perhaps
something about properties of magnets

we'd been studying in science class. We parroted
their talk about *AA12 step AA12 step on the wagon
stepped on the wagon 7 years on the wagon.*

THERE'S NO GOING BAREFOOT HERE

On damp days my new regulation navy blue coat
smells wooly. It hangs heavy like a burden on my shoulders.

I skid the icy streets. The required brown lace up shoes
are clunky. There is no going barefoot here.

I am far from home. There, it is either near the beach
or next to the mountains. It is where everyone can read

Spanish street signs and knows how to eat an artichoke
and what to do in case of a smog alert or earthquake.

By now the elm trees lining both sides of Main Street
have shed their autumn leaves, leaving crooked branches.

I miss streets bordered by tall skinny palm trees, oleander
and jacarandas exploding lavender blossoms.

Connecticut feels cold even when the sun is shining.
Houses look alike. White shingles, dark green doors

and shutters, holly hedges. They are serious. My house
is stucco, swarming with magenta bougainvilla, dwarfed

by a towering eucalyptus whose scrolls of bark peels
decorate the grass and flower beds.

Older students predict there will be snow before vacation.
Ridicule and snide word travel fast after "Hono-Lulu"

tells a few classmates she's never seen snow.
I'm proud of Mary Louise who, even after the first storm,

keeps on wearing, during free time, her brother's crazy
wild Aloha shirts under her navy blue coat.

TAKING STOCK

Like old friends she greets
the vertical scar bisecting her belly
the drooping arm flesh
the rounding of her proud shoulders

remembering how it was
before those several losses.
She allows her toes to soften
against the warmed limestone

while toweling her legs, strong
despite blue spider veins
webbing her thighs.
She resolves once again

at the start of another year
to be a good listener
to stay away from sugar
to avoid bitter thoughts no matter what.

METAPHORS

The British sculptor Henry Moore observed
the curve of a woman's thigh
echoes the slope of a mountain,
her inner thigh a valley in shadow.

I, too, see metaphors.
My wrinkles remind me of windblown
ripples of Sahara sand,
blue veins on my hands braided

channels of the Yellowstone River,
moles on my back archipelagos
I've seen far below from an airplane.
Simple comparisons of pattern, line, color

become more complex when imagination
is unleashed and ignites.
Odd, but compelling, to link disparate
images from the enduring natural world

with parts of the body, knowing the span
of a human life measures immeasurably less
time than it takes a firefly's flash or a spark
from a fire to be extinguished by darkness.

AT THE MALL

Restroom disinfectant, movie popcorn
and perfume samples mingle with Muzak
and merry-go-round music.
Solitary people wave to children

of strangers riding zebras and tigers
and dinosaurs and turtles while
they go up 'n down, round 'n round.
Sheltered from sun and rain, families

picnic at heavy metal tables bolted
to tile floors that rubber soled shoes
streak and squeak. Kids play video games
for exercise and quench their thirst

with sodas poured by the push of a lever.
Competing stores celebrate holidays
long before the season. Christmas trees
light up in early November. Easter bunnies

decked out in pink and blue satin bows
fill display windows by President's Day.
In late summer when kids go back to school
Halloween witches are riding their broomsticks

and displays of plastic pumpkins and bunches
of paper corn stalks made in China
decorate the mall before local farmers
harvest these same crops from their own fields.

NATURE'S WAY

She birthed her babies
this way. Pain forgotten at first cry.
And did it again four times.

She's ageing proud.
Wrinkles, white hair,
honorable knees that no longer
jump her into or out of bed.

She believes Botox poisons.
Tucking and lifting flesh a crime
against whom she was made to be.

She wouldn't consider buying
a grocery store spring bouquet
of dyed green and blue daisies.

A DAY BEGINS WITH AN 8.8

A loud rough voice wakes her out of a dream.
She sits up. The bed is bucking as if a pair

of elephants were on it making love.
The walls, tinged pink from parking lot lights,

sway in opposition to the moving bed. The counter
forces throw her down. She hears the roar of lion.

Bending knees to her chest she buries her head
under the pillow, searching a maternal breast.

Two hands grab her shoulders.
The same voice shouts *Get Up.* She sits up, again.

The TV, mirror, table lamps, water pitcher and glasses
are smashed on the tile floor.

She tries to make sense of it. Has an angry dragon
escaped from the fiery center of the earth? Are rhinos

clashing horns down there over a female or territory?
She remembers her husband. He must be somewhere.

They'd decided the comforter on the bed was heavy
for Santiago in January. It was still neatly folded

on the armchair, but now the armchair blocked
the way out to the hall.

The large photograph over the bed she'd admired
was askew. The wide blue cloudless sky was tilted.

The peaks of the Andes were pointing toward the door
instead of up to the cracked ceiling.

THE MARRIED

They study the world map
pasted on the wall.

Pushpins mark their travels.

Blue river lines wind through
countries with outdated borders.

New countries are missing.

Looking through photo albums
they question and quibble.

Blue Mosque or Sultan Mosque?
Neither she says.

The Tetons?
Not jagged enough he insists.

Together they count white crosses.
Punch Bowl? Normandy? Arlington?

Too many graves
Too many wars

They do agree.

LOST IN THE CAMERA'S EYE

Mom wanders

Age-spotted hands lightly brush framed photos
on tables around her house.

I follow

In one photo she stands beside a topiary duck,
smiling from under a wide brimmed straw hat.

I prompt

Your honeymoon? Chateau Villandry?

In another she and my dad lean against
a wood railing, the ocean behind.

I suggest

a favorite beach or two.

I point

to another. It's me holding my granddad's
big warm hand. His stiff white hair is tangible too.

She sits on his other side. We are under the arbor
he built himself, white lattice laced with blue morning glories.

Who

she asks?

Later, she unpins her bun and brushes her hair
with deliberate care in front of her bedroom mirror.

I ask

who do you see?

She does not answer.

This causes me to wonder
which might it be, habit or vanity,
that outlives self-recognition.

MRI

I see the image of my husband's brain. The doctor
points to a small white circle with a long Latin name.

It is floating in grey like a full moon waiting
for a blue dawn. Thoughts ricochet.

Leonardo Da Vinci dissected the human brain
in search of the seat of man's soul.

The old Mayan woman in Guatemala hid her face
afraid my camera would steal her soul.

On TV a man from Cleveland claimed he saw
his wife's soul leaves her body the moment she died.

And what about musical prodigies or preschoolers
able to solve algebraic equations? Are they old souls?

Are old souls different from the rest of us
who falter through our one life?

I saw the green flash from a boat in the Galapagos.
In the split second the sun slipped below the horizon

had I blinked I would have missed it. Wide-eyed now
there is no missing.

THIS IS ELEANOR

. . . happy as a cupcake in a frilled paper cup . . .
Janet Fitch, White Oleander

She is wearing
a starched organza dress
frosted with blue forget-me-nots.

We are party guests
in her fancy French house.

parquet floors
pretend Louis XVI chairs
tasseled silk pillows
arrayed on loveseats

a baby nurse upstairs
a manservant down
a husband around
who when spoken to smiles

I pay attention to her.

pretty
natural blonde
dainty feet
thick ankles
small waist
wide hips
matching pink
lips and nails

Her diamond decorated fingers
gesture when she speaks.

Fingers that before mine pressed
against my husband's naked back.

LINGERING

He sleeps curled on his right side,
a new position after the stroke.
Early mornings I slide across
the cool sheet to press my body
against his warm back.
Beneath blue striped cotton I thread
my left arm under his left arm.

I crawl my fingers over his body
seeking those damaged muscles
deep down in his side.
I want to find them, to know
their tightness as he does.
My hand lingers over his heart beat
and the silences in between.

AFTERMATH

Barbie appeared
with an alligator tattooed

on her shoulder.
A woman from Ohio

found a bent fish hook
in her tuna sandwich and

the Virgin Mary was seen
reflected in a storefront window

in downtown Tuscaloosa.
It seemed as if

after nine eleven
anything was possible.

A young man
strolling the green

of his neighborhood park
in Brooklyn discovered

the piece of litter he picked up
was a business card, charred

but legible, belonging to a friend
he'd not heard from.

WE ALL WILL RECEIVE

Passing someone on Fourth Street
I hear *sure is a nice mornin'*.
I notice the sun catches the light
hair on his legs and look up to see
his smile, a nice one, and reply *sure is*.
A reply not me but I want
to acknowledge the way he speaks,
want to be his friend, if only
for this moment. A grey bag slung
over his blue shoulder doesn't seem
a heavy load. I envision the stacks
of envelopes that bulge the canvas.
Fat thin rectangular square
each envelope bringing the expected
or unexpected, depending.

A18954

I recognize her
in the checkout line
from the jacket
of her memoir

coiffed curly brown hair
high cheekbones
half-smile on thin lips.

I follow her gaze
to the magazine rack
to the airbrushed starlets
tattooed rock stars
the 31 lb. chicken
on the cover
of the *National Enquirer*.

I glance in her grocery cart.

a bunch of carrots
a dozen eggs
a jar of strawberry jam
2 boxes of Kleenex
a bag of tangerines

She is like
any other shopper,
like me.
I have tangerines in my cart.

Yet who would know
she has witnessed

a newborn cradled
in his mother's arms
shot point blank.

She smells the smoke
after all these years.

She bears a tattoo
beneath the sleeve
of her ordinary blue blazer.

SOUP TUREEN

We never used the *don't touch* tureen
for its intended purpose. In our family
we ladled soups and chowders straight
from the cookpot. The tureen, older
than any relative on our family tree,
stayed put on the hall chest of drawers.
The blue Delft design was as traditional
as shrimp gumbo. Mom holding tight
to the acorn shaped knob would lift the lid
to reveal her cache of old necklaces.
The purple, green, and gold glimmer
of throws, parades, and her dancing days.

PRESSING FLOWERS

Aunt Sally taught me to press wild beach roses
and purple and white iris that lived at the edge
of island woods where we picnicked.
The hens-and-chicks growing on the rock wall

bordering her drive were too juicy. Fern fronds
and Queen Anne's lace pressed well, but clustered
petals of loosestrife found all over fell apart
with the lightest touch. Bushes of blue thistles

thicketed behind her house. I used sharp loppers
to cut a single head with three silver leaves
from the tough stalk. Aunt Sally helped me place
the prickly globe between sheets of wax paper.

I carefully lined up the wood squares of the press
before tightening down the corner screws.
The thistle would not flatten. *Stubborn* she said
won't yield. Tells us some things aren't meant to be.

CAUTIONARY TALE

When family visited Aunt Mimi and Uncle Bill
they shared the dusty living room. Otherwise,
they lived separately in opposite ends of the house.

Aunt Mimi wore her food stained raincoat every day,
sandaled feet sticking out below the hem, each toe
a red beacon of nail polish slathered to knuckles.

Every day Uncle Bill mowed the lawn surrounding
their house, his riding mower and he inseparable
as the Lone Ranger and Silver. During visits we kids

would follow his lizard tongue poke first one sunken
cheek and then the other. *Restless anger* Mom said
same as her swearing like a drunken sailor.

Late one summer night their house caught fire.
Uncle Bill escaped. Aunt Mimi did not. She'd fallen
asleep smoking in her curtained canopy bed.

Not surprised said Dad *my sister always* smoked *like
a chimney.* Uncle Bill proclaimed *she'd burned in hell.*
To be safe, he switched from Camel Blacks to Camel Blues.

BETWEEN THE PULLMAN CARS

When the stranger leaned over I saw a bird's nest
of braided hair coiled atop her head. She dangled
a twisted rope of red licorice in front of my face.
I broke off a piece and chewed. I knew that was wrong.

The slide and grind of metal floor plates opened
and shut like hungry scissors under my feet.
I remember how ankles overlapped her large
blue shoes. She asked my name but I didn't tell.

I spit the red wad into my hand, rolled it to a ball,
and dropped it into the gravel blur between the plates.
It was difficult with slimy palms to push against
the crossbar on the pressurized door but I did it.

GRIT STORIES

Nan

tells me on my visit to wish her a happy 93rd
birthday *just a couple of hundred pages to go
in my book*. Later that day her son found her
with the book face down on her lap, page 85
dog-eared, tinted blue glasses resting useless
beside an empty glass, nearby.

Michelle

on hot days wore her red and blue ski cap.
It's icy in that treatment room she explained.
Before the start of the season she bought two
ski passes and sharpened the edges of her skis.
Christmas morning her grandson found a card
in his stocking. *Give the extra to a friend* it said
I'll be looking down from the summit.

Anna

would ask me to press the inside of a banana peel
hard . . . harder against her forehead.
A strange request but it soothed the pain
living in her brain. Some days on the way
to chemo she sang parts of her favorite
"Blue Moon" or "Tea for Two." Other days she recited
backward and forward multiplication tables
because she'd read numbers were the last to go.

Richard

bought himself a new set of golf clubs
for his 87th birthday, confident they would help
lower his handicap. However, there wasn't time

to try. He put a note for his grandson
in a side pocket of the golf bag. On a scrap
of paper in a scribble of blue it read *I waited
too long. Good luck.* He must have been in a hurry
because he left the pen in the pocket with the note.

Sara

pushes open the clinic door, reluctant to leave
the reassuring warmth of one more morning.
Nothing has changed since the last time I came
with her. The linoleum floor is still flecked brown
and grey. The rows of blue recliners continue
to face each other. Glass bottles hang from the same
menacing metal stands.

She slips on a heavy sweater, her wool cap
and socks and waits for the nurse's weekly search
for a usable vein. When time's up she changes
from battle fatigues into a hot pink sundress
and matching shoes, just right for South Florida.
She combs and fluffs her thinning curls before leaving
the hostile air-conditioning.

Jeanette

had always fancied herself alluring. In spite of
90-year-old knobby hands and withered breasts,
she still did. Her great-grandson's wedding was to be
celebrated in nearby Sioux City on Valentine's Day.
In August she began a study of fashion catalogues
in search of something just right. It took several months
to find the blue lace waltz length dress she ordered.
Then she waited. A few days before Thanksgiving
the package arrived. The postmaster, whose father
had been Jeanette's all through high school sweetheart,
with regret stamped it *Deceased/Return to Sender.*

KNOT BOARDS

My cousin Kath and I practiced tying knots
on our boards while Uncle David observed
our fingers follow his intricate instructions.

Buoy Hitch
Anchor Hitch
Half Hitch
Slip Knot
Figure-eight . . .

He did not show us.
We had to listen.
This was part of the learning.

On a Sunday morning years later
with the awaited birth of her first grandchild
Kath decided, at the last moment,

to skip church with her husband.
Alone at home she must have removed
the single strand of cultured pearls

she always wore with church clothes
before lowering the loose noose knot
of braided blue nylon rope over her head.

SEA GLASS

In the hunt for glass shards polished smooth
by shifting sand of winter storms
our small eager fingers twisted into
rock crevices risking barnacle cuts.

Light green and beer bottle-brown
were common as sand fleas.
The blue of Grandmother's tear drop bottle
of Midnight Velvet prized.

Summer's end Grandfather summoned
all cousins to the dock for the ritual throw-back.
He tallied in his notebook the plink plinks
as each piece of glass fell into the water.

We asked ourselves why does he count or care.
One year someone dared to ask.
Important he said *to keep an accurate record
of all treasures found or let go.*

KATH'S CROOKED FINGER

Kath was the first of the cousins to read.
She would read aloud to the rest of us
who couldn't.
With her crooked pointer finger
(jammed in a slammed drawer)
she would follow the words
and, in our favorite story, the route
up up and over
the mountain of the little engine,
who puffing clouds of blue smoke,
said *I think I can I think I can*
until he could.
If Kath saw something of interest
outside the picture window
she'd point *look*. Because her finger
bent to the left all we could see
was the empty corner of the room.

PRALINES

My sister and I count the days
until Uncle Hugo arrives.

He turns our family routine
upside down, every which way

which gives leeway and latitude
to our expected behavior.

When he arrives we watch
while unpacks his tote bag.

With exaggeration he plunks
down the contents on the counter.

A sack of shelled pecans
halves or pieces . . . either'll do

two blue and white boxes of sugar
gotta be Godchaux

a bottle of vanilla
real stuff . . . bought it in Guadalajara

and a candy thermometer
which he unwraps carefully

because he knows after opening
every kitchen drawer last year

that we didn't own one.
Stumped, he'd made it clear

next year I'm bringin' my own fixin's.

PROFESSOR M DISMISSES CLASS EARLY

Professor M announces rhythmic
possibilities of poetry will be the day's topic.
However, she changes course, meandering

her Nebraska 4-H youth, 3 advanced
degrees, 2 chipped molars (the upper right
hurts) and Ted, a grad student she seduced

(not at this university.) She reads one
of her autobiographical poems
to illustrate syllabic verse. It is a narrative

that rambles as long as the road trip
it describes. There's explicit love making
with mustachioed Charlie in cheap motels,

a lot of tequila with Tex-Mex food, and tumble
weeds blowing across every back road. Weary
of reading her own creation she stuffs notes

and class handouts into her leather bag
and flounces her blue gypsy skirt out the door
heading, it appears, southwest toward El Paso.

BROWN

I follow Darlene into the coffee shop.
Her blonde hula skirt hair

sways across bony shoulders,
her torn blue jeans and black sweater

shapeless off her stick figure body.
Today Darlene revealed herself in class.

In her sonnet she described a girl
who would eat only foods that match,

one color for each meal.
I watch her cut a sliver

from a packaged brownie and nibble it
with her coffee. When I ask her

about the sonnet
she assures me *that was a long time ago.*

TIGHTNESS SQUEEZES A FRIEND

like an old fashioned
whale bone corset.

She sweeps mealtime crumbs
before the last bite

makes beds
before sheets cool

replaces light bulbs
hot to the touch.

lines up spices ABC
anise basil cumin

shelves shoes by color
black above brown below blue.

BEFORE MY TIME

Jim's escapades and eccentricities
are the stuff of local lore.

He sailed his sloop to Key West

and back again to Maine with his wife
and year-old daughter safe
in a hammock slung across the cabin.

He spent a winter

in an abandoned cabin on Birch Island
sculling to the mainland only when
drinking water and kerosene ran low.

He claimed to have survived that winter

on peanut butter and jelly sandwiches,
William Shakespeare, Dylan Thomas,
and learning to play the ukulele.

The following year he traded his PhD

and tenure for a used McCormick dozer
and began clearing stumps and dead trees
beside family summer cottages.

It is said he created a maze of footpaths

through the woods at the end of the road.
The paths, like Jim, are gone, overrun by
trillium, barberry and bittersweet vines.

IN THE KENTUCKY SCIENCE MUSEUM

a teacup found several miles
from the *Titanic* rests upon

soft folds of blue-grey velvet
in a display case. A line of gold

traces the rim and handle formed
to fit the delicate grasp of elegant

fingers. The flawless porcelain
glaze is pristine white from years

of saltwater washings. Reminiscent
of penne pasta, six white worm-like

creatures cling fused to the inside
curve, a place of refuge.

On the wall behind the display case
a photograph captures the teacup

in situ. Here, it rested upon the seabed
before discovery, pluck, and plunder.

THE AUNTS

Aunt May, by all accounts, no matter what, refused to leave her house on Friday the thirteenth. During hot weather she refrigerated her lipsticks, little metallic tubes shelved beside her favorite blueberries and farm fresh eggs. In winter she slept under a mink coat just like Aunt Ann the year she studied sculpture in New York and lived with her Aunt Mary. She slept in a clawfoot bathtub covered with one of her aunt's castoff furs. I love the photo of Aunt Jo, my dad's favorite sister, swathed in the sheared beaver coat Aunt Betsy gave her before she moved to St. Croix. Aunt Jo's cat Bob was a tortoiseshell whose coat swirled orange and brown. He spent his days in her kitchen on the counter next to the stove with his right eye open.

ELEGY FOR A BLUE AND WHITE SCHWINN

You have labored muddy trails
freewheeled ocean boardwalks
threaded traffic with bravado.

Skittering driveway gravel
like a crab in a hurry
you would come back home.

This time like a millstone or nuisance
my daughter is leaving you behind.
Your Texas Longhorn handlebars

will rust. Spider webs will choke
your spokes. Your tires will deflate.
No turning now.

WILKES

His mother, my daughter,
labors hard to push him

out and into the morning
of the first day of the first month

of the new year. I witness
his birth, hear his first cry.

A declaration.
I am here!

I count silently. He is flaw-
less, glazed with vernix

like the snowy world outside.
The nurse selects the blue blanket

swaddles him and lays him
beside his mother.

I am unable
to find an adjective adequate
to describe his birth.

wonderful   (too trite)
awesome   (too trifling)
miraculous   (too tame)

EPITAPH

The receptionist at the hair salon raises
her arm reaching for the appointment book.

I notice black lines etched into the mocha skin
of her upper arm. They form a face that moves

and alters with the motion of her arm.
Inked teeth skew to parallelograms. Nostrils shift

from round to oval. Curls covering the head
seem to bounce. Her arm pushes with familiarity

against her ample bosom while scanning the list
of appointment times and names.

Her sparkly blue fingernail searches and finds me.
I debate, but have to ask whose face it is.

The sparkly blue points to beneath the chin.

Mother 1952-2008

DRESS UP CLOSET

It would be possible to reorder
from left to right
with some historical accuracy
old family clothes
hanging in the dress up closet.

Gran's black sequined flapper dress
Yale Class of 1928 reunion blazer
WWII Navy uniform
Pink poodle skirt with 45 record appliqués
Korean War Army sergeant's uniform
Polyester bell bottom pants
Vietnam tropical combat jacket
blue leather mini skirt

Somebody's tweed coat
with a *To Hell with Beef Where's the Lobster?*
button fastened to the lapel
could fit in most anywhere.

BLUE DRESS IN JOHANNESBURG

They say the countryside was painted blue.
Government issued blue tarps covered mass graves.

I picture the spared ones, grieving and angry, digging
through skulls and bones with sticks and long brown fingers.

But how would a mother know her child? A son his father?
A brother his sister? And on and on.

Here is what I've seen. A no frills dress. About size 4
with short sleeves and scoop neck. It is displayed

on an ordinary clothes hanger in the Constitutional Court
art collection. The dress overshadows portraits of Mandela

and other anti-apartheid leaders, overpowers
life size bronze sculptures of stooped and weary miners.

The simple design is waterproof, durable, and blue.

BLACK DRESS

When my dad turned 85
I decided my blue dress
with plaid cuffs might not be properly

proper. I should buy, just in case,
a simple black dress to be ready.
I was sure I'd be busy deciding

which Bible readings and prayers
and hymns and who would sit
in which pew with whom. I anticipated

greeting his friends and accepting
each *I'm so sorry* and *we'll miss him.*
There would be no time to think about

what to wear or to pay attention
to the hole that had already
begun to dig itself into my heart.

TIGHT PASSAGE

The curved wall and wrought iron banister
prevent clear passage, the stretcher too stiff
to maneuver the narrow twist of the stairs.

I suggest the two men from the funeral home
fashion a hammock from your top bed sheet,
the one with Mom's initials monogrammed in blue.

One man at your head, the other at your feet.
I am in the middle, stepping sideways
to cradle your body, to steady the swing.

It's the first time I have carried you, Dad.
You are heavier than I expected.

BEYOND THE THREE-MILE MARK

We cast off.

The port of San Pedro recedes, diminishes
and disappears behind the wake.
Beyond the three-mile mark Captain Dave
cuts the motor. We drift tame swells.
The Pacific is living up to her name today.

My thoughts wander.

I imagine Dad's gold fillings buried
in his ashes like plastic babies hidden
in Mardi Gras King Cakes,

the flowers we intend to throw
like doubloons tossed from floats
parting the crowds along Canal Street.

I am back.

We hold hands to recite

the Our Father
the 23rd Psalm
the prayer of St. Francis.

It is time.

I scatter his ashes.
My daughters throw azalea blossoms
they have picked from his garden.

The reds and pinks and whites
bob and dip the spreading grey stain
until there is only a blue amen.